PREFACE

Dvořák's *Stabat Mater*, his first setting of a religious text, was begun in February 1876 in memory of his daughter Josefa who died in September 1875. In August 1877 another of Dvořák's daughters, Ruzena, died followed by his first-born son, Otaker, in September. It was in the wake of these events that Dvořák completed the score of the *Stabat Mater* in the October and November of that same year. The work did not receive its first performance until 23 December 1880 in Prague. In 1883, it was performed in London with such success that the composer was invited to conduct it himself in 1884. This was the beginning of Dvořák's popularity in Britain.

The score was published in 1881 by Simrock, presumably under the composer's supervision, and this version is the basis of the present edition. In 1883, Novello published a vocal score, with an organ accompaniment arranged by H. E. Button and English words by F. J. W. Crowe. In 1904 a further vocal score was published by Novello, with Button's organ accompaniment arranged for piano and the original Latin words.

The *Stabat Mater* text is attributed to Jacopone da Todi, and is almost certainly a thirteenth century Franciscan composition. There is no authorised version of the *Stabat Mater* as there are for other liturgical texts. In one place the variations between versions of the *Stabat Mater* text have given the composer the opportunity for extra text. This occurs in the fourth stanza of the text used in the first movement of the work. Some sources give the second line of the fourth stanza as 'Pia mater, dum videbat' while others give it as 'Et tremebat cum videbat', the latter being followed by many composers, though with seeming indifference over the position of the words 'cum' and 'dum'. Dvořák happily uses both lines (making a five line stanza) and is also unconcerned about the use of 'cum' and 'dum'. This is understandable, since the words can be used interchangeably in some contexts, as can 'when' and 'while' in English. Since there does not appear to be any particular purpose in this variety, this edition uses 'dum' after 'Pia mater' and 'cum' after 'et tremebat' throughout. Footnotes indicate where this differs from Simrock's full score.

Michael Pilkington
Old Coulsdon
November 1999

****

This new edition of the *Stabat Mater* follows the layout of the previous edition (catalogue number NOV 070090) page for page, to allow this new edition to be used side-by-side with the edition it supersedes.

T0052967

STABAT MATER

Stabat mater dolorosa
juxta crucem lacrimosa,
dum pendebat Filius.

A mother stood grief-stricken,
by the cross, weeping,
while her son was hanging there.

Cujus animam gementem,
contristatam et dolentem,
pertransivit gladius.

As she shared in his sorrow
And grieved, a sword
Pierced her groaning heart.

O quam tristis et afflicta
fuit illa benedicta,
mater unigeniti.

O how sorrowful and afflicted
was that blessed woman,
the mother of the only-begotten one.

Quæ mærebat et dolebat,
pia mater, dum videbat
et tremebat cum videbat
nati pœnas incliti.

Devoted mother, who mourned
and grieved while she saw,
who trembled,
seeing the punishment of her glorious son.

Quis est homo, qui non fleret,
matrem Christi si videret
in tanto supplicio?

Who is the man who would not weep
if he saw the mother of Christ
in such torment?

Quis non posset contristari,
Christi matrem contemplari
dolentem cum filio?

Who could not share in the sorrow,
were he to contemplate
the mother of Christ grieving for her son.

Pro peccatis suæ gentis
vidit Jesum in tormentis
et flagellis subditum.

She saw Jesus in agony
and subjected to whips
for the sins of his nation.

Vidit suum dulcem natum
moriendo desolatum,
dum emisit spiritum.

She saw her sweet child
desolate in his dying moments,
as his spirit slipped away.

Eia mater, fons amoris,
me sentire vim doloris
fac, ut tecum lugeam.

Alas, mother, fountain of love,
let me feel the force of your grief,
so that I may bemoan with you.

Fac ut ardeat cor meum
in amando Christum Deum
ut sibi complaceam.

Let my heart burn
with love of Christ our Lord
so that I may please him.

Sancta mater, istud agas,
crucifixi fige plagas
cordi meo valide.

Holy mother, do just that,
let the blows of the crucified one
drive strongly into my heart.

Tui nati vulnerati,
tam dignati pro me pati,
pœnas mecum divide.

Share with me the punishment
of your wounded son
who suffered so worthily for me.

The New Novello Choral Edition

ANTONÍN DVOŘÁK

Stabat Mater

for soprano, alto, tenor and bass soloists, SATB and orchestra

Vocal score

Revised by Michael Pilkington

Order No: NOV 072503

NOVELLO PUBLISHING LIMITED

It is requested that on all concert notices and programmes acknowledgement is made to 'The New Novello Choral Edition'.

Es wird gebeten, auf sämtlichen Konzertankündigungen und Programmen 'The New Novello Choral Edition' als Quelle zu erwähnen.

Il est exigé que toutes notices et programmes de concerts, comportent des remerciements à 'The New Novello Choral Edition'.

Orchestral material is available on hire from the Publisher.

Orchestermaterial ist beim Verlag erhältlich.

Les partitions d'orchestre sont en location disponibles chez l'editeur.

Permission to reproduce from the Preface of this Edition must be obtained from the Publisher.

Die Erlaubnis, das Vorwort dieser Ausgabe oder Teile desselben zu reproduzieren, muß beim Verlag eingeholt werden.

Le droit de reproduction de ce document à partir de la préface doit être obtenu de l'éditeur.

Cover illustration: first page of the autograph score of Dvorák's *Stabat Mater* (courtesy of the Muzeum Antonína Dvořáka, Prague).

© Copyright 2000 Novello & Company Limited

Published in Great Britain by Novelle Publishing Limited
Head Office: 14-15 Berners Street, London W1T 3LJ
Tel +44 (0)20 7434 0066   Fax +44 (0)20 7287 6329

EXCLUSIVELY DISTRIBUTED BY

HAL•LEONARD®

All rights reserved   Printed in Great Britain

Music setting by Stave Origination

No part of this publication may be copied or reproduced in any form or by any means without the prior permission of Novello & Company Limited.

Ohne vorherige Genehmigung der Firma Novello & Company Limited darf kein Bestandteil dieser Publikation in irgendeiner Form oder auf irgendeine Art und Weise kopiert bzw. reproduziert werden.

Aucun partie de cette publication ne pourra être copiée ni reproduite sous quelque forme que ce soit, ni par quelque moyen que ce soit, sans l'autorisation préalable de Novello & Company Limited.

Fac me vere tecum flere,	Let me truly weep with you,
crucifixo condolere,	grieve with you for him, crucified,
donec ego vixero.	for as long as I live.

Juxta crucem tecum stare,
te libenter sociare
in planctu desidero.

I long to stand by the cross with you,
gladly keeping company
with you in your lamentation.

Virgo virginum præclara,
mihi jam non sis amara,
fac me tecum plangere.

Virgin, most noble of virgins,
do not now be bitter towards me,
let me lament with you.

Fac, ut portem Christi mortem,
passionis fac consortem,
et plagas recolere.

Let me bear Christ's death,
let me share in his sufferings
and receive the blows.

Fac me plagis vulnerari,
cruce hac inebriari,
ob amorem filii.

Let me be wounded by the lashes,
intoxicated by that cross,
through love for your son.

Inflammatus et accensus,
per te, Virgo, sim defensus,
In die judicii.

Blazing and scorched,
may I be protected by you Virgin,
on the day of judgement.

Fac me cruce custodiri,
morte Christi præmuniri,
confoveri gratia.

Let me be guarded by the cross,
defended by the death of Christ,
fostered by grace.

Quando corpus morietur,
fac, ut animæ donetur
paradisi gloria. Amen.

When my body has died,
let it be that the glory of paradise
is granted to my soul. Amen.

Translated by Emma Marshall

STABAT MATER

STABAT MATER DOLOROSA

© Copyright 2000 Novello & Company Limited

4

6

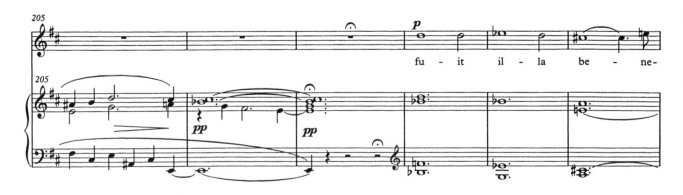

12

14

* cum = dum in FS

* dum = cum in FS

18

* dum = cum in FS

22

23

24

QUIS EST HOMO

28

32

36

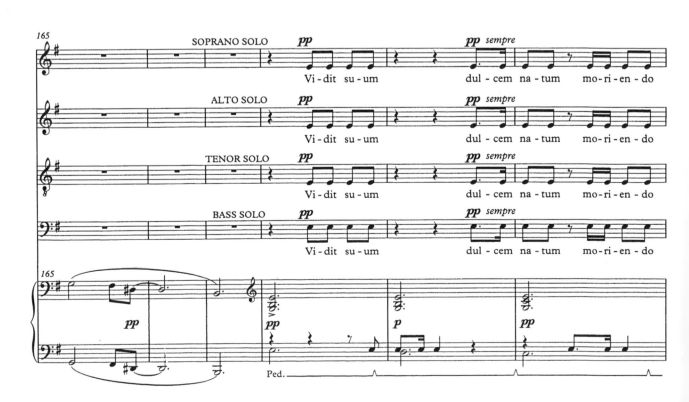

EIA MATER

40

FAC UT ARDEAT COR MEUM

48

50

TUI NATI VULNERATI

Andante con moto, quasi Allegretto (♩. = 42)

56

58

FAC ME VERE TECUM FLERE

64

66

70

VIRGO VIRGINUM PRÆCLARA

* cue-sized notes for rehearsal only

* for rehearsal only

72

* for rehearsal only

* for rehearsal only

74

76

FAC, UT PORTEM CHRISTI MORTEM

INFLAMMATUS ET ACCENSUS

QUANDO CORPUS MORIETUR

94

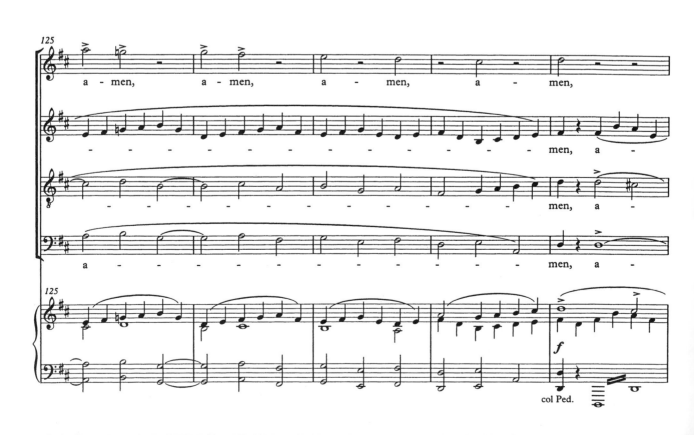

* for rehearsal only

-ne - tur pa - ra - di - si, pa - ra - di - si glo -

-ne - tur pa - ra - di - si, pa - ra - di - si glo -

-ne - tur pa - ra - di - si, pa - ra - di - si glo -

-ne - tur pa - ra - di - si, pa - ra - di - si glo -

- - - - ri - a.

- - - - ri - a.

- - - - ri - a.

- - - - ri - a.

molto tranquillo

104